CONTENTS

CD TRACK LISTINGS

With Lyrics

1. Blue Star
2. Funny Little Star
3. Cotton Wool Clouds
4. Hello, It's Me!
5. The Star of Bethlehem
6. Inside a Stable
7. Every Star Can Shine
8. Every Star Can Shine (Reprise)

Instrumentals

9. Blue Star
10. Funny Little Star
11. Cotton Wool Clouds
12. Hello, It's Me!
13. The Star of Bethlehem
14. Inside a Stable
15. Every Star Can Shine
16. Every Star Can Shine (Reprise)

TEACHER'S NOTES

Young children of every ability and confidence level can join in the fun with this simple and flexible musical. There is plenty of scope for adaptation to the needs of your group or class.

This musical can be performed either by large groups of children of one or more classes combined, or by smaller groups with some children playing more than one part. Teachers, helpers and willing parents can also get involved. Where appropriate, the spoken parts can even be incorporated into the narration, which can then be read out by an adult, leaving the children free to enjoy singing the songs. The opportunity to cut the play or to add your own ideas is freely available.

It requires minimal costumes and props and the accompaniments can be played on a piano, keyboard or guitar, or simply use the C.D. in a stereo system or player.

'The Little Blue Star' can be used in many different ways to explore a variety of different topics:

- The Nativity Story and its role in the Christian faith
- Religious, cultural and seasonal festivals and their symbols
- Differences and similarities; individual, social, cultural
- Travel – finding out about other countries, where they are and how far away they are
- Meeting new friends and learning about new people and places
- Welcoming a new baby
- Dance, movement and physical expression
- Counting, shape sorting, colour and shape recognition
- Comparative and superlative language
- Art and Craft projects

CHARACTER LIST

Narrator	A confident child speaker, teacher or parent is needed to tell our special story. Can also be split between several speakers.
Singers	This can consist of the children in the play and/or a separate group placed to one side.
Stars 1, 2, 3, 4, 5	A bit of acting required with a couple of lines to learn and lots of fun dressing up.
The Little Blue Star	The leading role. A self assured and expressive little girl would be perfect for the star of the show!
Clouds 1, 2, 3, 4, 5, 6, 7, 8, 9	With just one line each but plenty of bouncing, rushing and gliding, these parts are great fun to perform.
Bethlehem Star	A confident youngster would suit this part. Some acting is needed to show sympathy to The Little Blue Star and to portray the importance of the special job he must do.
Kings 1, 2, 3	Each has just one line to learn and where numbers are limited, they could play other characters as well.
Shepherds 1, 2, 3	As with the kings, the shepherds have just one line to learn and where numbers are limited, they could double up as other characters also.
Mary & Joseph	The only non-speaking parts but still essential to our Christmas story.
Baby Jesus	The little baby can be played by a favourite dolly, safely wrapped in a soft blanket or shawl.

STAGING IDEAS

Your sets and props can be as simple or elaborate as you like. There is no formal set as such but the children may enjoy painting a backdrop of the night sky in dark blues and purples then painting or pasting on glittery stars. The only furniture required is a small crib for the baby Jesus and a chair each for Mary and Joseph, to be placed to one side.

Use the following as guidelines that you can freely adapt or add to as you wish:

Stars 1, 2, 3, 4, 5	White or silver outfits decorated with plenty of glitter and sparkle. Silver tinsel headdresses are easy to make and can be used on their own where costumes are limited. Little wands with stars on one end, perhaps with silver streamers attached to portray the beauty of the stars in the night sky.
The Little Blue Star	A blue outfit with blue tinsel, sequins and glitter would be stunning for our heroine.
Clouds 1, 2, 3, 4, 5, 6, 7, 8, 9	White costumes, perhaps using lengths of white muslin or netting that the children can twirl and wave during their performance.
Bethlehem Star	A yellow or gold outfit with masses of gold sparkles of every sort – glitter, sequins, tinsel, whatever you can find. A star headdress cut from card and coloured gold would make this special star stand out.
Kings 1, 2, 3	The children can make crowns during a craft lesson and also have fun making 'jewels' that could be glued to lengths of velvet or dark material to portray cloaks.
Shepherds 1, 2, 3	The classic tea-towel with a headband is always a favourite choice for shepherds. Failing that, a simple t-shirt and trousers in earthy/brown colours. They carry a soft toy lamb, a small blanket and a lantern.
Mary and Joseph	A coloured cloak or length of material round the shoulders – blue is traditional for Mary.

SCRIPT AND SONG LYRICS

Narrator: One night, a long, long time ago, a new star appeared in the sky. All the other stars twinkled and shone. They filled the universe with their beautiful gold and silver lights. But the new star was different, because this star was blue.

Song 1 - Blue Star

1. Blue star, blue star dancing in the sky
Blue star, blue star dancing up high
Little star new, little star blue

2. Blue star, blue star floating in the sky
Blue star, blue star floating up high
Little star new, little star blue

3. Blue star, blue star sparkling in the sky
Blue star, blue star sparkling up high
Little star new, little star blue

4. Blue star, blue star twinkling in the sky
Blue star, blue star twinkling up high
Little star new, little star blue

Narrator: The other stars didn't want a blue star for a friend and they all made fun of her.

Star 1: You're a funny star!

Star 2: You're all blue!

Star 3: That's a silly colour!

Star 4: We don't like you!

Star 5: Go away blue star!

Song 2 - Funny Little Star

1. You're a new star, you're a blue star
And you don't belong with us!
You're an odd star, being blue, star
You're a funny little funny little star

2. You're a new star, you're a blue star
And we want you to go away!
You're an odd star, being blue, star
You're a funny little funny little star

(Instrumental – during which the other stars whisper to each other behind their hands, making fun of her and giggling. The blue star looks miserable and hangs her head.)

3. You're a new star, you're a blue star
And you don't belong with us!
You're an odd star, being blue, star
You're a funny little funny little star

Narrator: Little Blue Star felt very sad. She said goodbye to the other stars and went away all by herself into the big, big universe.

She flew slowly along through the night sky, hoping to find a friend. But there was nobody and she didn't know where to go or what to do.

She floated around in the universe for days and days. Then at long last she looked below and noticed some white, fluffy clouds. They bounced through the sky and sang a song.

Song 3 - Cotton Wool Clouds

1. Bouncing, bouncing, bouncing through the sky
Bouncing, bouncing, bouncing as we fly
Light as a feather, cotton wool clouds

2. Rushing, rushing, rushing through the sky
Rushing, rushing, rushing as we fly
Light as a feather, cotton wool clouds

3. Gliding, gliding, gliding through the sky
Gliding, gliding, gliding as we fly
Light as a feather, cotton wool clouds

4. Bouncing, bouncing, bouncing through the sky
Bouncing, bouncing, bouncing as we fly
Light as a feather, cotton wool clouds

Narrator: The little blue star flew after the bouncing clouds.

Little Blue Star: Will you be my friends?

Cloud 1: We're too busy!

Cloud 2: Busy, busy!

Cloud 3: Bouncing!

Cloud 4: Rushing!

Cloud 5: Gliding!

Cloud 6: Drifting!

Cloud 7: Floating!

Cloud 8: Flying!

Cloud 9: *(or all)* Too busy, too busy!!

Narrator: So off flew the bouncy clouds.
As they flew away, Little Blue Star could see something in the distance. It was Mother Earth. The earth looked friendly.
She decided to float all the way down to say hello to the Earth.
Down, down, down she went to say hello to the Earth.

Song 4 - Hello, It's Me!

(Can be sung by just The Little Blue Star or all the children)

1. Hello, it's me, Little Blue Star
Hello, it's me and I have travelled far
Hello, it's me, Little Blue Star
Hello, it's me and I have travelled far
I'm here to see if you will be friends with me
Can I stay with you?
Do you mind that I'm blue?

2. Hello, it's me, Little Blue Star
Hello, it's me and I have travelled far
Hello, it's me, Little Blue Star
Hello, it's me and I have travelled far
I'm here to see if you will be friends with me
Can I stay with you?
Do you mind that I'm blue?

3. Hello, it's me, Little Blue Star
Hello, it's me and I have travelled far
Hello, it's me, Little Blue Star
Hello, it's me and I have travelled far

Narrator: As the Little Blue Star came closer to the earth she heard a big voice from behind the mountains.

Bethlehem Star: I am the Star of Bethlehem. I will be your friend and take care of you.

Narrator: The great big shiny Bethlehem Star rose up from behind the mountains.

Song 5 - The Star of Bethlehem

1. He is a shiny star, he is a shiny star
He is the Star of Bethlehem
He is a shiny star, he is a shiny star
He is the Star of Bethlehem

2. You can go and follow him
You can fly along with him
Through the sky to Bethlehem
He will be your own starry friend

3. He is a noble star, he is a noble star
He is the Star of Bethlehem
He is a noble star, he is a noble star
He is the Star of Bethlehem

4. You can go and follow him
You can fly along with him
Through the sky to Bethlehem
He will be your own starry friend

5. He is a shiny star, he is a shiny star
He is the Star of Bethlehem
He is a shiny star, he is a shiny star
He is the Star of Bethlehem

Narrator: The big star told the Little Blue Star why he had to go to Bethlehem.

Bethlehem Star: A special baby is born in Bethlehem. He is the saviour of all the world.

Narrator: The big star said that three mighty kings were going to see the baby. Some shepherds would be going too. So the Star of Bethlehem had to shine very brightly to show everyone the way.

The big star took the Little Blue Star by the hand.

Bethlehem Star: Would you like to help me?

Little Blue Star: Yes please!!

Narrator: They floated all the way to Bethlehem and stopped over a stable. There inside the stable they saw Mary, Joseph and the baby Jesus.

Song 6 - Inside a Stable

1. Inside a stable, under a star
There was a baby born
A tiny child asleep and warm
Asleep and warm

2. Inside a stable, under a star
There was a baby born
We stayed and watched until the dawn
Until the dawn

3. Inside a stable, under a star
There was a baby born
A tiny child asleep and warm
Asleep and warm

Narrator: As the Little Blue Star watched, three kings came to see the baby. They gave him precious gifts.

King 1: Gold for the baby.

King 2: Frankincense for the baby.

King 3: Myrrh for the baby.

Narrator: Shepherds brought lambs and other gifts.

Shepherd 1: A lamb for you.

Shepherd 2: Something to keep you warm.

Shepherd 3: A lantern for you.

Song 7 - Every Star Can Shine

(Sing Twice)

Jesus is born, Jesus is born
Under the stars that shine above
Jesus is born, Jesus is born
Under the stars that shine above
Every star can shine
Every little star can shine tonight
Every star can shine
Because it's Christmas time

Narrator: From far away the other stars could see the bright light of the Star of Bethlehem. They floated down to the stable where Jesus lay. They were surprised to see the Little Blue Star there.

Star 1 *(or 6)*: Why is Little Blue Star here?

Star 2 *(or 7)*: We don't like her, she's different.

Bethlehem Star: You are mistaken, little stars. She is special, and so are you.

Narrator: The Bethlehem star spoke in a big loud voice to all the night time stars. He told them that Jesus says we are all as important as each other and special in our own way.

They all felt very sorry.

Stars: *(Walking across to stand with The Little Blue Star)*

Please can we stay with you Little Blue Star and watch the baby Jesus?

Narrator: The Little Blue Star forgave all the other stars. Together they watched the manger scene and sang their Christmas song.

Song 8 - Every Star Can Shine (Reprise)

(Sing Twice)

Jesus is born, Jesus is born

Under the stars that shine above

Jesus is born, Jesus is born

Under the stars that shine above

Every star can shine

Every little star can shine tonight

Every star can shine

Because it's Christmas time

Blue Star

♩ = 98

Happily

Words & Music
By Niki Davies

17
Bm7 E7 A F♯m Bm7 E7 A
Lit - tle star new, lit - tle star blue.
Lit - tle star new, lit - tle star blue.
21
Dmaj7 Amaj9
25
Dmaj7 Bm7 E A Bm/A
3. Blue star,
29
Amaj7 A Bm/A Amaj7 Bm7/A A Bm/A
blue star spark - ling in the sky. Blue star,

33
Amaj7 Bm/A Amaj7 Bm7 E7
blue star spark - ling up high. Lit - tle star
37
A F♯m Bm7 E7 A
new, lit - tle star blue.
41
Dmaj7 Amaj9
45
Dmaj7 Bm7 E A Bm/A Amaj7
4. Blue star, blue star

49
A Bm/A Amaj7 Bm7 A Bm/A Amaj7
twink - ling in the sky. Blue star, blue star
53
Bm/A Bm7 E7 A F♯m
twink - ling up high. Lit - tle star new,
57
Bm7 E7 A Bm7 A
lit - tle star blue.

Funny Little Star!

Words and Music
By Niki Davies

♩ = 122
With purpose

2.
15
Am7 D7 G D7
20
G C G
24
G
3. You're a new star, you're a blue star, and you
27
D7
don't be - long with us! You're an odd star be - ing
30
G/D C/E G C G
blue, star. You're a fun - ny lit - tle, fun - ny lit - tle star.

Cotton Wool Clouds

Words and Music
By Niki Davies

♩. = 90

Bouncy!

14
G7
C
Gm7
C
Gm7
feath - er, cot - ton wool clouds.
17
1.
2.
Dm7
G7
Dm7
G7
21
smoothly
C
Gm7
C
Gm7
C
Gm7
3. Glid - ing, glid - ing, glid - ing through the
smoothly
24
C
B♭
C
Gm7
C
Gm7
C
Gm7
sky. Glid - ing, glid - ing, glid - ing as we

28
C Bb Dm G7
fly. Light as a feath - er, cot - ton - wool
31
C Gm7 C Gm7 Dm7 G7
clouds.
35
C Gm7 C Gm7 C Gm7
4. Bounc - ing, bounc - ing, bounc - ing through the
38
C Bb C Gm7 C Gm7
sky. Bounc - ing, bounc - ing,

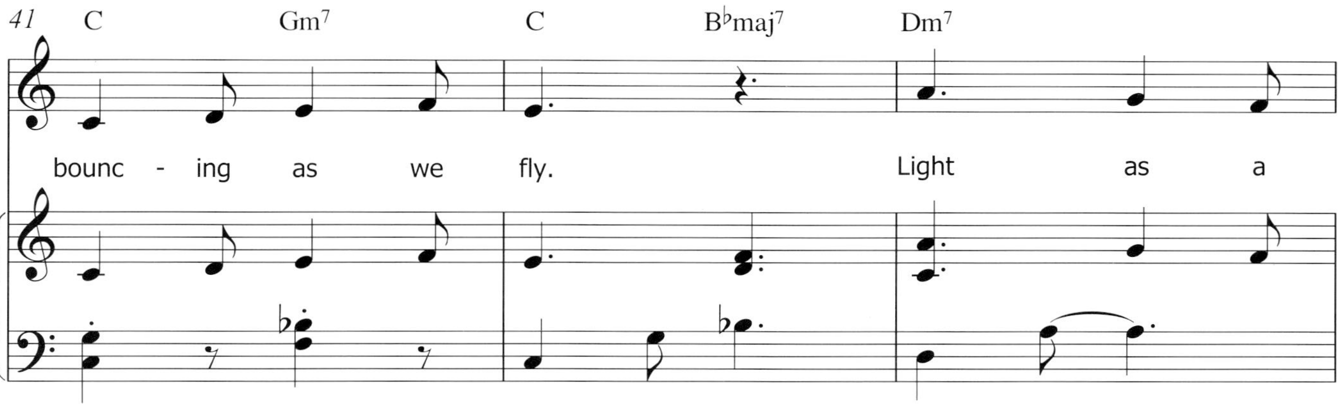
41
C Gm7 C B♭maj7 Dm7
bounc - ing as we fly. Light as a

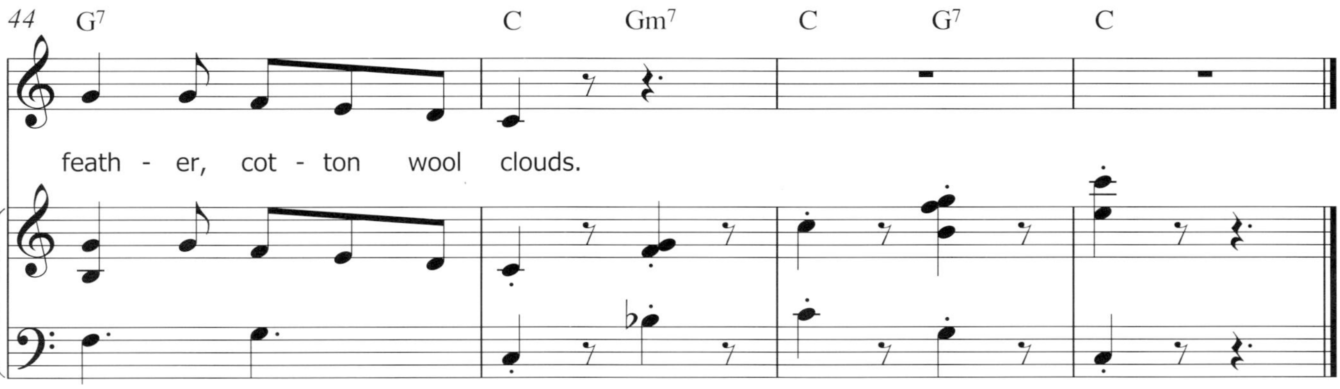
44
G7 C Gm7 C G7 C
feath - er, cot - ton wool clouds.

Hello, It's Me!

Words and Music
By Niki Davies

♩ = 118

Brightly

rall
17
G A7 D Bm7 E7
Can I stay with you? Do you mind that I'm
rall
a tempo
20
Asus4 A7 D Em7 A7
blue? Hel - lo, it's me, Lit - tle Blue Star. Hel -
a tempo
23
D G A D
lo, it's me, and I have trav - elled far. Hel - lo, it's me,
26
Em7 A7 D G A D
Lit - tle Blue Star. Hel - lo, it's me, and I have trav - elled far.

Star Of Bethlehem

Words and Music
By Niki Davies

15
Gm7 C7 F Dm7 Gm7 C7
You can fly a - long with him. Through the sky to
18
F D Gm7 C7
Beth - le - hem, he will be your own star - ry friend.
21
F B♭ C7
3. He is a shin - y star, he is a shin - y star, he is the Star of
24
F C7 F B♭ C7 F B♭ F
Beth - le - hem. He is a shin - y star, he is a shin - y star, he is the Star of Beth - le - hem.

Inside A Stable

Words and Music
By Niki Davies

2.
F Fmaj7 Gm7 C7 F
dawn. 3. In - side a
Fmaj7 Gm7 C7 Gm7 C7
sta - ble, un - der a star, there was a ba - by
F F7 B♭maj7 G7 F
born. A tin - y child, a - sleep and
D7 Gm7 C7 F Gm7 F
warm, a - sleep and warm.

Every Star Can Shine

Words and Music
By Niki Davies

♩ = 160

Brightly

25
Bm7 E7 Amaj7 F#m7
Ev - ery star can shine,
30
Bm7 E7 Amaj7 F#m7 Bm7
ev - ery lit - tle star can shine to - night. Ev - ery
35
E7 Amaj7 F#m7 1. Bm7
star can shine be - cause it's Christ - mas
40
E7 2. rit Bm7 E7 A D/2 A
time. Christ - mas time.
rit

CURRICULUM LINKS

Song 1 — Blue Star

Knowledge & Understanding of the World:

Ask the children what they know about stars. Where are stars? Are they above us or below us? What else is above us? What things might be below us?

Science:

Talk about the night sky. Explain that blue stars are new stars. They are millions of years old instead of billions of years old like our sun. Describe how blue stars are actually hotter than red stars.

Creative Development:

Create a picture of the night sky, encouraging the children to explore different materials such as tin foil, glitter, potato prints, fabric etc.

Physical Development:

Play the music CD and ask the children to dance and move like The Little Blue Star – making shapes with their bodies and moving as if floating, sparkling and twinkling.

Mathematical Development:

Repeating patterns – use foam or cut potato stamps to make repeat star patterns as Christmas decorations, cards or wrapping paper

Song 2 — Funny Little Star

Personal, Social & Emotional Development:

Talk about how The Little Blue Star is being treated by the other stars. Use circle time to think about how The Little Blue Star feels. Have they ever felt like that? Write a 'code' as a whole class. How would the children treat The Little Blue Star if she joined their class? What would she need to know about their school? Do the children think some things might be strange or unusual? How could they help her settle into their school and feel welcome?

Song 3

Cotton Wool Clouds

Knowledge & Understanding of the World:

Talk about clouds; where they are, the different colours and types – from fluffy white summer clouds to dark rain clouds and heavy storm clouds. Have any of the children ever been on an aeroplane and flown through the clouds? What did it feel like? What could they see?

Physical Development:

This song provides a great opportunity for the children to express themselves physically. Can they bounce like a Cotton Wool Cloud? Ask them to rush along then glide then bounce again. An excellent way to burn up some energy and for the children to practise their agility and control. Use ribbons, scarves, pieces of muslin or white netting to enhance the dance movements and represent the clouds.

Song 4

Hello, It's Me!

Communication, Language and Literacy:

Can the children write a class poem about The Little Blue Star or about meeting new friends for the first time? Develop a word bank of Little Blue Star words. This can then help them try to develop short poems of their own.

Personal, Social & Emotional Development:

Talk about making new friends and meeting new people. Ask them to think about all the different people there are in the world, the differences and similarities. Look at different types of clothes, languages, ways of living etc. Discuss 'What makes us special'. Use a classroom display based around The Little Blue Star to reinforce individual differences in a positive light.

Song 5

The Star of Bethlehem

Knowledge & Understanding of the World:

Ask the children to think about the important job the Star of Bethlehem performs. How does he show the way and how do the travellers know where the baby Jesus is? Where is Bethlehem? You can use this opportunity to show the children a map and discuss what it might be like to live in another country or to travel far away. Have they ever been to another country? What was it like?

Song 6

Inside a Stable

Personal, Social & Emotional Development:

Talk about the Nativity Story. Who is the baby Jesus? Do they know why his birth is important?
Have any of the children got baby brothers or sisters? What was it like when the new baby came? What do new babies need?

Song 7

Every Star Can Shine

Personal, Social & Emotional Development:

Use circle time again to talk about how the other stars change the way they treat The Little Blue Star. How do they think she feels now? What important lesson have the other stars learned? This is another good opportunity for the children to think and talk about accepting differences and feeling special. Use the classroom display from 'Hello, It's Me!' to follow up this theme.

Mathematical Development:

Give the children a selection of stars of different sizes and colours. Using 'smaller', 'bigger' language, ask which is the biggest star? Which is the smallest star? Can the children sort them into sizes from biggest to smallest, also using 'bigger than' and 'smaller than'? Now sort them into different colours. You could also mix the star shapes with various other shapes (circles, squares, diamonds, rectangles etc) and ask the children to sort them.

Song 8 — Every Star Can Shine (Reprise)

Communication, Language and Literacy:

In response to listening to and performing The Little Blue Star, can the children write a simple story about her? Can they describe what she looks like, how she sounds, what she does and where she goes? What happens at the end of the story and how does she feel? Use the word bank mentioned in 'Hello, It's Me!' to enhance and develop this activity.

Knowledge & Understanding of the World:

Think about stars at Christmas time. Why are they *used* to illustrate the festive season? Where else might we see stars used to signify a particular holiday or event? This would be a good opportunity to discuss other religious festivals that use stars or light to represent a special day.

LICENCE APPLICATION FORM

You will need a licence to perform The Little Blue Star to an audience (other than to children in your school and members of staff). To apply for a licence please photocopy this page, complete the details as necessary and send it to Niki Davies Productions Ltd at the address below. If there are any unique circumstances, which suggest that a licence would not be appropriate please contact us by phone for advice.

Licence rates:	1 performance (no admission charge)	£12.00	(inc VAT) *
	Additional performances (no admission charge)	£ 6.00 each	(inc VAT) *
	1 performance (with admission charge)	£18.00	(inc VAT) *
	Additional performances (with admission charge)	£ 8.00 each	(inc VAT) *

The above fees are applicable for 2005 and may be subject to revision.

We hereby apply for a licence to perform 'The Little Blue Star' by Niki Davies

Name of school/organisation..

Contact name... **Tel number**...

Invoice address..

....

....

Post code ....

Number of performances.................. **Admission fee charged?** Y/N (delete one)

Performance date(s)..

Payment options

☐ I enclose a cheque (pounds sterling only) in the sum of £ ....

☐ Please invoice my school at the above address

* A discount of 5% is applicable to applications accompanied by cheque

The licence also includes the right to reproduce the lyrics of the songs for distribution to the audience. However, all such reproductions MUST include the following credit: Reproduced by kind permission of Niki Davies Productions Ltd © 2005.

If recordings of the performance are made to sell to parents or to the public, please contact Niki Davies Productions Ltd.

Address: PC www.nikidaviesproductions.com 46 1718
La Email: info@nikidaviesproductions.com ›sproductions.com